Pimp Game 201

Exercising Your Knowledge of the Game

TJ Clemons

itbftr@yahoo.com

Introduction

It was my actual intentions to retire from the pimping game but due to

the current economic climate I had to come out of retirement and get

back to chasing paper. When it's all you really know how to do then it

becomes a natural thing to do. The same way that you never forget

how to walk or ride a bicycle. Because one thing I do know is that in

every financial condition pussy will sell. And a lot of professional

women are in need of management.

And since pimping is my specialized and preferred occupational

lifestyle then I have to get back out there and exercise my game and

bring some real pimping back into the game.

It was my destiny to get back into the game and take it to yet another

level. Although, I have made lots and lots of money over the years I

failed to invest my profits wisely. I had to learn a few new tricks in the

square world when it comes to multiplying your financial assets to

my advantage. So, I plan on getting out here and putting my pimping

back into practice for the next 3 to 5 years so that I can retire

comfortably without having to worry about any monetary issues.

I'm right back to square one but the good thing about me is that I

seriously believe in my pimping and that is the key to my ultimate

success and my ultimate victorious outcome.

Now let's begin my journey back into the game together because I

really enjoy writing about the game and putting it out into the world

for a small fee. Because as we all know game is to be sold not told.

It's all about applying your knowledge of the game into your own

individual pimping style. This is what separates you from the average

want to be pimp. Real pimps know how to pimp.

And all these other guys are busy watching, learning, and mimicking

real pimping. I was once doing the same thing until I learned to respect

the pimping game, studied it, and put it down like a man of leisure.

Real Pimping Put into Practice

I had a mother and my father and I learned from a young age that a

man was put on earth to get money from my father. He got down and

dirty in the dope game. I had an amazing childhood for the most part

during the 1980's and the 1990's crack era.

My neighborhood turned to shit quickly when crack cocaine started

booming. I quickly learned to turn to the streets for my income.

 In my personal opinion if you try to jump into the street life after 25

or 30 years old you're pretty much in the way of real street hustlers.

Whatever it is what you were doing before then you should pretty much stick to doing that square shit. I started off around 8 or 9 years old breaking into houses. Me and my cousin actually broke into the plugs house one time and he thought his girl set him up to get robbed and he beat her up real bad over that incident.

We climbed in through his window and we took all of his drugs and money. We actually heard her getting beat up and he definitely put in some work on shorty. Then from there it was whatever we could do to get some money while we out there in the streets hustling.

The game was always around me in various ways, shapes, and forms.

There are so many different kinds of underworlds when it comes to

the streets. You have people who steal cars, you have boosters,

drug dealers and so on and everybody moves in different circles and

the same circles at the same time. It's all about hustling and putting

your foot the grind to make that almighty dollar bill.

I started off selling dope and one of the old school players pulled my

coat and let me know that I could be doing other things on a whole

other level.

It wasn't like I wasn't making a whole lot of money at the time but he

started putting me on to the pimping game. It started off for me at

the strip club. I was having a little money in the dope game and my

pockets where pretty decent most of the time.

We were up in the strip club watching all these dudes making in rain in

the strip club basically blowing money fast on these females. And then

he pulled me to the side and said, "Let me talk to you young blood."

So, we sat there at the bar talking to each other the whole night.

It was a wild night at the strip club, watching these beautiful ladies do

there thing and get their paper all night long. So, I just sat there and

listened to what he had to say out of respect for him and his time.

All night long he talked about this and that, then at the end of the night

he kind of stopped talking about the jibber jabber. He was just really

stalling and then he broke it down to me telling me that, "Now this is

the good part." After he seen that I had the time and patience to really

learn about the game that he was about to put down on me then it was

time for him to put down the meat on the sandwich that I was about

to devour bite by bite.

It was a particular woman that a lot of men had been throwing a lot

of money at and he pointed her out to me. He said to me real slick,

"You see that pretty little lady over there? She is about to go over there

and give all of the money that she made out here shaking her pretty

little ass to that guy over. Pay attention son. This is the good part that I

have been waiting for you to see for yourself."

And I saw her walk smooth over there in her high heel stilettos and

pull out stacks of money and give it to him with a smile on her face.

And then he really broke down the game to me. He said to me,

"You see all these stupid mother fuckers give her all of that money?

They could have just cut out the middle man and just given their money

straight to him. Now, what's the difference between you and him?

You have all those girls coming to your house all day and night but

you're still out here hustling and running around with guns risking

your life for a little bit of bread. You need to chill the fuck out and

start moving different. I can feel the pimping in you young blood."

So, one day I finally took his advice and the rest is history.

It feels like a better lifestyle but nothing out here in the streets is safe.

That's definitely a misconception. Because a pimp is always in danger.

All these young guys want to be in the game because all they really

see is the glitz and glamour on the outside looking in.

They see the cars, women, and money which are all the irrelevant

side of the game. They don't see themselves as a target at all.

When I caught my case I was looking at 170 years.

How safe does that part of the pimping game feel?

I would have been better off shooting a few people and would have

been facing less time. I ended up doing 7 and a half years behind bars.

I transitioned into the pimping game in the early 1990's.

I was dibbling and dabbling at first in the 1980's. I had 3 solid females

out there getting money but I was still getting a lot of money in the

drug game. When I first started out that pimp game money didn't

really impress me. It was only when I finally starting focusing on the

game then I understood the concept of taking it to the next level.

Then the next thing you know you are living in a nice house filled

with the most exotic and luxurious things that money can buy.

I had to have the most outlandish and unique things which also gave

me the ability to attract beautiful women that wanted to be a part

of this glamorous lifestyle and experience with a man like me.

It basically came with the territory. It was all about living life to the

fullest at 100 miles per hour every day in the fast lane.

Guys like me really did it when we were doing our thing as real

mother fucking pimps. I'm what they call an original gangster.

I'm basically a dinosaur in the game. I'm retired now.

A lot of these young guys are running my old plays.

Back when I was heavy in the game I wore a lot of nice clothes

fur coats, and jewelry. I also had a lot of luxury cars and traveled

across the country city to city and spent a lot of time in various motels.

I'm 55 years old but that's old in the street game because a lot of

the people that I ran with didn't make it to see 40 years old.

I got shot when I was 19 years old so I'm blessed to still be here.

So, I'm basically a senior citizen in the streets. So, many people

that I was around died in their early 20's both family and friends.

A lot of people don't make it to this age from the streets.

I dealt with a gritty reality. Everything was right there in your face.

The blocks that I grew up on were notorious for crime and everything

else under the sun. There was a lot of brutality on a daily basis.

It was a different reality for us at that time.

Everybody wasn't getting money like I was getting money so it was

basically a mother fucking rat race. There were only actually a very

select few that was actually getting any real money so everyone else

was eating off of us in some way, shape, or form.

The streets were full of wolves and lions and there was a fine line in

between the haves and the have nots so anything could jump off at any

given time in that concrete jungle because people always wanted what

you had and some of them would do just about anything to get it if

they were given the opportunity to do so.

So, to wear diamonds, jewelry, and drive nice cars you had to be a

certain kind of guy out in the streets. You definitely had to know how

to carry yourself. You couldn't be soft while you're getting money.

Flashing and flossing in the face of everyone is basically enticing that

hunger inside of them. You can't keep waving a steak in front of wild

animals and not expect that something could possibly happen to you.

You can't walk around with a gun in your hand all day every day.

People are going to think that you're scared and eventually

somebody is going to try you just to see what you're about.

I basically only wore jewelry when I went out to the clubs but I also

made sure that I had a gun stashed somewhere close by just in case

something went down. I remember going to hide my gun behind a

dumpster and it was already two pistols back behind there.

That was how we had to move back then though just to go to a

night club. But you never knew when a shootout would or could

breakout. Somebody is always beefing. It's just a matter of when

and where that it ends up going down in the streets. That was just

the everyday reality of growing up in the hood lifestyle.

The game has changed over the years. I don't even respect what they

call pimping now. I'm pretty much cool on it. It's sad what is going on

right now. I say that because when I was in the game we all had love

for each other and we were all out here getting money.

There was a lot more money floating around. Even some people that

we considered as being "broke" had a decent cash flow. There wasn't

as much disrespect going on. These new pimps go around dissing each

other because basically they are gang members hustling these women.

These females are on so many drugs that their habit takes up a lot of

their money just to keep working every day. And then they don't really

do anything for the females. They barely even feed them anything but

drugs. In my day your women were always your status symbol.

If you were a high level asset out here then they could tell by how good

that you took care of your women. Your main woman had to be

something different, beautiful, and exotic.

We were out there moving and grooving and we had our women

looking like movie stars jumping in out of luxury cars. I remember some

guys having Porsches and Rolls Royce's. The men and women both had

on full length mink coats and real diamonds and jewelry.

They looked like the wives of professional athletes and movie stars.

Now these females look like junkies and don't even have on clean

clothes most of the time. They are seriously giving the pimping game

a black eye and a bad reputation.

I have yet to see a movement of these new guys out here

actually caring about what they are doing. Now it's all about being

loud, annoying, making noise, and disrespecting pretty much everybody

that they come in contact with on a daily basis.

I don't even understand why they are even in the game. Everyone is

basically broke and struggling to make it day by day.

A lot of these young dudes reach out to me and ask me to mentor them

and I really don't want to waste my time and energy if they really aren't

serious about it because I have other things to do with my time.

But there a chosen few that I actually see that have the potential to

really do something in the pimping game. So, I take some time and give

them some real information. I even tell them a little bit about investing

some of their money into crypto currencies.

It's a smooth hustle instead of just spending all of your money everyday

and waking up the next day trying to pay for a motel room just to keep

a roof over your head. You definitely have to invest some of that bread

into something that has some kind of potential to fall back onto

when times get rough.

A few hundred dollars can potentially turn into a few thousand dollars

very quickly if you keep putting money into that grind on a daily basis.

You really have to have your mind on the future instead of expecting

something to happen every single day.

I definitely put them up on the financial side of the game. You have to

think about every aspect of getting money and making that money

work for you on several different levels.

The game is cute but you have to know how to manage money or

you're just hustling to survive. Even when I was locked up mother

fuckers on the inside was trying to learn about pimping.

I would always give it to them real and raw. First of all I had to let

them know the reality of the shoes that they wanted to step into.

And I would always asking them if they knew the punch line of the

joke that they were asking me was.

Take a real good look at where both of us are right now. We are sitting

in prison. This situation that I was currently locked up in put a lot of

stress on me as well as my family.

I had a kid that was born while I was locked up. I couldn't be there for

him as a father the way that I wanted to be. Now I'm sitting in there

thinking about what was really important to me.

Fuck the money! Fuck the cars! Fuck everything!

Those things don't really mean anything in prison. Now all I have to

worry about is getting this bullshit commissary every week.

Snacks are the currency in prison. Food is money.

Somebody will fuck you up over some 25 cent ramen mother fucking

noodles! It's a whole different world and reality inside of the prison

industrial system.

And you have to mentally prepare yourself for entering back into the

free world. All you had to get by on at that point was letters and

pictures from your woman who has been fucking everybody else while

you are away on this fucked up vacation from society.

Prison wasn't fly at all. I had to decide whether or not I was going to go

back to pimping or try to live a square life. This was a major decision

that was going to affect the rest of my natural life.

Some dudes are even trying to find a place to live when they get out.

Luckily every penitentiary has a pen pal system where you can hook

up with a female from the outside world that is looking for a man

fresh out of prison system. So, if you have a little bit of game then

you're going to be fine. This is basically pimping on a different level.

They even have tablets inside and if you have a girl on the outside sending you money then networking is that much easier. You can have your main girl on deck and have a few females on the side as backup plans just in case baby girl was selling you a dream and she is living with a mother fucker already and she is just using you as her fantasy man behind bars. Females are known to play these kinds of games so you have to play your own game of survival.

The whole mother fucking time she might be sending you money,

letters, and sexy pictures and she is hiding all that from her man

at home. So, you better have a fat girl on your team that is more

than willing to take care of you when you come home.

That pimping and prostitution game is still on the internet. You might

even find a woman that is willing to put in work for you and help you

get your money up. Just be careful how you move or you might end up

right back in a cold dark place far away from home. Make sure that

she is all the way down for you before you make that chess move.

Always remember the women around you are there to represent you

to the mother fucking fullest. So, she has to be looking good.

Looking beautiful gives women more confidence about their

appearance. And an attractive women is sought after more aggressively

by men with money which automatically increases her value financially.

It is just a good business practice to upgrade your woman as much as

possible because in turn the money that she can potentially generate

will also increase in worth that much faster.

Money makes money so you have to look at her as an investment in making money and attracting other female followers to you.

You and your woman are the trend setters. Both of you are working together towards a common objective which is getting real money.

You have to be able to separate yourself from the pack.

You have to look like you're doing big things. Fake it until you really make it if you have to. It's part of the grind. You will eventually move forward and progress if you put your mind to it.

Even in a recession pussy will sell. You just have to put her in a position

to win with your pimping. You wouldn't believe what you could make

happen if you push her in the right direction.

It's an everyday hustle and grind to improve on your pimping.

It's a learning experience that can be financially beneficial for you.

You have to move at your own pace to learn how to win at your level.

It's a mental game. You have to help her to overcome any obstacle that

is going to come her way.

You send her out there with the right information and instructions to

come back with as much money as she can with less and less effort

over a period of time. That's real mother fucking pimping!

They have this thing called making a quota every day. As long as they

make one thousand dollars daily they are satisfied and happy.

Then they blow $600 for hotel rooms, food, and drugs.

After that then they might send the females out again after they

threaten to beat them up. I didn't really have to put my hands on a

woman unless she got out of pocket and I had to put her back in line.

And that was on a very rare occasion to let the other bitches know that

I was not a game to be played with. And I might have slapped her one

good time because I really didn't want to mess up her face because

that was going to mess up my money. Most of the time I used mind

games on them because I knew that if they feared me then they

would respect my pimping. It really isn't necessary to beat a woman

up all the time because that really made me look bad as far as I was

concerned. That was what we called running out of pimping.

You look dumb as fuck if you have to beat a bitch up all the time to

make her act right. One of my mentors told me that if you didn't have

to beat the bitch up to get her out here then you shouldn't have to

beat her up for her to have to do what she has to do for you as a man.

I always went by that concept. So, if you always have to choke her out

or put your foot up her ass then you're running out of game too fast.

Females are emotional creatures and you have to know how to play

on her emotions. It's all about controlling her mind instead of her body.

She is a representation of you and your pimping.

She is under your authority and control.

So, if you beat her the fuck up, then you're messing up your own

pockets. It's basically not a good look. There isn't any real prestige or

honor in that as a man. And you don't get any points for that.

Your game is fading away. The game is being run by these low-level

street hustlers. Let's be honest. But the game will never go away.

Prostitution is not the game. Prostitution is the act of females doing

what they have to do while they are out there in honor of the game.

The game is the game. It has rules and principles.

Prostitution will always be around but it's not the game. The game is

when you take a female or a set of females and you put them in the

presence of their king. You basically put some queens with a king.

They are not always queens when they first show up and choose him.

Kings make queens. A queen can be a common woman until she

marries a king. Then they become married to the game.

Because an empire cannot be ran successfully without a king.

Any real chess player knows that all the queen's moves are in

protection of the king. And if you move the pawns forward successfully

then you can have as many queens on the chess board as you want.

These women come as pawns and you make them into queens.

But these so called pimps now find them where they are and destroy

these females until they are pretty much useless.

They really aren't trying to build their brides up in the game.

They really aren't trying to build a real relationship, future, or

foundation together as a productive unit.

They are just trying to get as many females as they can under one roof

and run it like a halfway house. They are basically housing females.

They don't have any real direction. I wasn't raised in the game like that.

You're always supposed to able to sustain a household and a bankroll

for every female. You are the manager of the bills and everything that

is going on with every player on your team.

I moved totally different. I was way more organized within my own

organization. Just like on every professional team the players don't

go home together. But we did play together successfully.

We showed up at the game. We play our asses off. Then we go home to

our separate residences so that we can live our lives. So, when we show

up at the game we are all ready to play our positions as a team.

A lot of time in sports the team members don't even get along with

each other. Kobe and Shaq didn't really see eye to eye but when they

got together they won championships. I don't really have to be your

friend to win with you.

A lot of these dudes are more interested in what it looks like from the

outside than what it really is on the inside. They would rather look good

on camera more than they do in real life situations.

I tell these youngsters all the time that my real life is way better than

the one that you made up on Facebook and instagram. And a lot of

them just don't grasp that concept at all. Pimping is about seeing the

 results of your actions instead of pretending to be something that

you really aren't.

That's a façade and a make believe world and real women just aren't

going to respect that especially if they are looking for real pimping and

knowledge in this game.

I don't really give a fuck about what people think about me.

I say what I feel. If it's real to me then it's real as far as I'm concerned.

A lot of these dudes are just a part of the pack. They aren't real kings.

They just go with the flow as long as the money is coming in.

I live by the code. You don't tell on your friends. You don't betray those

people that have been loyal to you and you make sure that everybody

around you eats the fruit of their labor.

This is the mother fucking game and the code of the streets. You have

to live by some kind of basic principles. I remember when pimps had

fly cars, clothes, and they were icons. The real drug crews were teams

and everybody had money.

One man can't sit at the top and have everybody around him struggling.

How the fuck does that look? That's not a strong team. That's a strong

individual. My uncle taught me that. He starved the whole team.

Then on the other side there was another crew. And they looked totally

different when they pulled up. They took care of everybody around

them. They were like Big Meech and BMF. Everybody was looking good

and shining like new money.

And the people in my uncle's crew got played and shorted on money.

And they couldn't afford nice cars or to do this and that. And I could

see how much better the winning team looked in comparison.

And from then on there I knew in my heart that I had a much better

chance if I treated my people right and created loyalty on my team.

That's that big me little you mentality and that is exactly what brings

down empires. You have to remember when you grow up from nothing

in the hood not having things that you work that much harder when

opportunities are given to you to become successful.

The game is a tool not a career. It's that catalyst that is supposed to

take you to the next level. It's a foundation for you to stand on.

A lot of people don't even have the mindset to even want to move

up or elevate beyond what they are already doing on a daily basis.

It's all about your level of gratification and satisfaction because some

people are cool just being mediocre and living a status quo lifestyle.

You have to know and understand the reality of your overall situation

in order to become greater than you already are as a pimp in this game.

Don't expect anything out of your circumstances if you're not building

yourself up and applying yourself in the principles of learning the ins

and outs of the pimping game.

If you don't know how to treat your females then you're not going to

get much out of them if you're not constantly building their confidence

up and having them look like movie stars.

All they are basically doing is beating her up and taking her money.

That's not real pimping at all. She is going to end up going to the police

and putting a domestic violence case on you when she gets fed up.

You're going to be locked up calling baby girl a snitch when you wasn't

treating her like a real woman that was helping you to get your money

up out here. She is 120 pounds and terrified of you and she knows that

the only way to get away and get you out of her life is to put a case on

you so that she can move on to a better situation.

She knows that those badges and guns can get you the fuck away from

her because she is sick and tired and getting a foot in her ass after

putting of her hard earned money in your mother fucking pockets.

Your dumb ass is taking care of business and you're fucking up the

money instead of managing it. She is tired of walking around all the

mother fucking time because you don't have a car.

Any bitch in her right mind is going to give up on a mother fucker that

has her out here struggling and barely keeping a roof over your heads

when she is breaking bread with you.

Your job as her pimp is to manage the money and every situation

correctly as her man. You have to be an asset instead of a liability.

Because a bullshit situation is eventually going to play itself out.

You got all these clothes, shoes, and jewelry and no mother fucking

money in your pockets and she is walking around with a black eye

and a busted lip. Make it make sense to me young player.

So, that basically leads to an indictment and incarceration for you

while she seeks a better life for herself with somebody with a better

pimping strategy.

These females aren't slow but your played out game is for sure.

Now here you are talking down on the bitch when you wasn't handling

your state of affairs correctly as the manger.

That's exactly how a mother fucker gets fired from their position. That's

why there are so many renegades out here because these bitches don't

want to fuck with the bullshit mother fuckers calling themselves pimps.

Most females want a good man in their corner but if you're not helping

the circumstances then you're hurting the situation. You have to be

that right gentleman to step up and be able to handle everything for

her the way that it needs to be taken care of. That's what being a pimp

is all about. You have to be there for her when nobody else can or will.

These females can tell by your track record and what you have done

in order for them to figure out if they want to keep fucking with you

or not. You can't sell a dream to a mother fucker who doesn't even

believe in you or recognize that you're a good overall investment in

her future well-being as a queen.

Then you have a lot of females out here as renegades and outlaws

outside of the game doing what they do without any real guidance

or direction in life. They are just out here doing their own thing.

There is a difference between a renegade and a female who just

doesn't want to fuck with just anybody. She just hasn't found anybody

that's genuine and that is going to have her back out here that she sees

a bright future with.

Some women leave the last pimp that they were with and just end up

doing better by themselves. Then they might get with the next mother

fucker and they might end up losing everything that they built up on

their own hard work and dedication to the prostitution game.

Some of these dudes can't even do something with a motivated

female because they lack the vision and overall understanding of the

game. They tend to have that all on a bitch mentality and that is just

not how the pimping game goes because she is looking for you to

teach her something new and tighten up her game.

They keep blowing all the money and not spending it wisely and then

they just keep sending her out there to get more money without

getting any results or advancements for her to stay motivated.

The sad part is that there are way too many females out here that

accept that and they really call that pimping now. They are basically

just going in a big circle to nowhere. Nothing is actually getting done.

They might end up finally getting a raggedy car or an apartment

together but that's basically it. Any square mother fucker can

accomplish that or do better in reality. She is making just enough

money for him to ride around all day doing nothing so he can pick

her up from the track. That sounds like the movie Baby Boy to me.

Another thing that I keep hearing about is that these new pimps

are giving his new girls the old clothes like hand me downs from

his other girls. These females really need to know their value.

Because if you don't know your value as a woman then you will

basically settle for anything. I know my value a king and that's

exactly why I choose not to settle for just anything.

I come from a mean bloodline. The men in my family were hustlers.

The game has changed a lot from what I can see and not all for the

better. Your overall hustle and discipline is what separates men in the

pimping game. You have to first of all be knowledgeable about the

game and you also have to know to innovate and improve on your

strategy as time goes on and the world around you changes daily.

These new dudes are always in a rush to show off. Myself personally,

I came into the game with luxury cars with booming stereo systems.

But before I had any real money I had discipline. I remember sleeping

on the park benches and riding the subways in New York all night long.

People use to make fun of my lifestyle at the time. I was cool with my

situation at the time because I had a plan. I had a little bit of money

in my pockets at the time but I knew that I needed that money to make

other moves. I wasn't in a rush to move too fast.

I knew people back in the day that saved up thousands of dollars just

to buy jewelry. Then they bought that expensive jewelry and just ended

up being broke again and they had to start over from scratch.

Jewelry wasn't that serious to me. I like making money and being able

to stack money. Because when opportunities present themselves to

me I want to be able to jump on them and capitalize on those types

of situations efficiently and effectively. That's real hustling to me.

Because when you have all of those nice clothes, cars, and jewelry it

doesn't really show people how much money you have. What it actually

shows them is how much money that you have blown on material

things that don't really mean anything. Too many people are out here

breaking their necks to buy things that they really can't afford.

The game is broken right now. There is no code, morals, or values,

These young dudes are screaming out shit like:

"We don't love these hoes!"

So, why are you out here trying to pimp them then?

Because obviously these so called hoes love you or they wouldn't be

out here selling their bodies and bringing their money back to you.

They are trying to live the façade of being pimps. You can't pretend to

be a pimp. Either you're a pimp or you aren't a pimp. Make it make

sense to me young blood because you can't have it both ways.

That's like being a drug dealer and saying that you don't like drug users.

This is your way to make some decent mother fucking money.

Then you're out here physically and mentally abusing your source of

income. It's a dysfunctional pattern. But it probably started off from

their childhoods and households.

Some of these mother fuckers are probably crack babies though,

 because they were all pretty much born in the crack era.

They were conceived with that poisonous mentality in their system.

Most of their parents weren't around to properly raise them.

They come from broken homes and the foster care system.

They were raised with pain and abuse and all they really know how

to do is give it back to these females who are desperately trying to

love them. The problem then has no choice or other option but to

repeat itself and move on to the next generation like a curse.

These parents are dying off in this generation rapidly from drugs,

disease, and all kinds of destruction. It's a fucking epidemic.

I was raised in the golden era of everything music and culture.

Our senses of values have pretty much left. It's just not here anymore.

All everybody out here does is do drugs, shake their ass, and kill

each other. That's what this new generation is doing.

They idolize the shooter, when the shooter is just a pawn on the board.

The king isn't out here shooting people. The shooter isn't getting any

real money. And I don't want the shooter hanging around me.

I'm going to give the shooter whatever he thinks his life is worth to

go handle some business for me. There is no real honor in being the

mother fucking shooter. I grew up in the era that bred men in the

boss mentality. We emulated the boss image.

These mother fuckers in this era are walking around weird ass fuck.

They are drug users and junkies. And they have these females out

here getting money and bringing it back to mother fuckers with habits.

You have to have some kind of discipline. That's what's fucking the

game up right now. Without discipline there is disrespect, anarchy,

and no kind of real order.

Going to prison taught me that. I'm actually glad that we have a prison

system because there are some mother fuckers that belong behind

bars for the rest of their lives because they have done some weird shit!

There absolutely has to be discipline, law, and order in this world.

Being a drug addict is the norm. It's all in the music and culture.

So, the game is becoming a product of that mindset.

You are the product of the books that you read and the people that

you surround yourself with. And most people don't read books

anymore. They get their information from the internet and social

media. That's what they call the news now.

That's what validates their life and existence. And that is exactly why I

don't pay any of that much attention. I keep myself rooted in reality

because when your reality is solid then that other shit is irrelevant.

I don't drive rental cars around pretending like they are mine.

I don't do dumb shit like that. And I don't mistreat my females.

That was never my thing when I was in the game. Every woman

that I dealt with in the past still fucks with me. We're still friends.

We still call and check on each other from time to time.

I'm still interested in what's going on in their lives because that time

that we spent together way back when meant something to me.

She was a significant piece of building the empire that we had.

Just like a profession athletic team. We had our dynasty and we

won championships together and eventually we moved on.

We still have that bond and all those memories together.

That love and respect is still present today.

These young dudes need to learn what to place value on. And because

of their attitudes they will never experience the kind of success that I

had out here in the pimping game or have the money that came my

way. Because once you have everything that you ever wanted or

experienced in life money becomes irrelevant.

Going to prison really taught me what was valuable. I had to see my

children grow up through pictures. I lost loved ones to death that I will

never see again when I finally got back home. Those are the things that

no amount of money can buy or replace.

That is what life is really about knowing what is valuable and has real

value. Once you learn that then you learn what to not hold in high

regard. You learn what not to place so much time and energy on.

If you're a stand up dude then you have the best interest in mind

for the people around you. You don't shit on your friends.

And you don't fuck over the people that are loyal to you.

I use to have a rule: Which was simply spoil the loyal.

When you're that type of individual life treats you good.

You end up having a lot less regrets in life.

Life is a roller coaster and you have to enjoy the highs and the lows.

You learn from your mistakes and become a better version of yourself.

If you're the same man that you were at 30 that you were at 20 then

you wasted 10 years of your life and so on up the ladder in your life.

It's a growing process and it makes you the man that you are in life.

That's how you get your values and your principles.

I remember my father and step father got into it when I was younger.

They ended up pulling out guns on each other. It was a very intense.

They had their pistols locked and mother fucking loaded.

My pops did everything in his power to protect me from getting shot.

At one point he got in between me and my stepfather.

And then he told my stepfather to go ahead and shoot him.

My pops wouldn't fold for shit and he was willing to take that bullet.

It really taught me something that day.

My pops was ready to die for what he believed in.

And he put his life on the line to protect me.

He kissed me one last time not knowing it could be his last time.

But when that dude seen how far my father was willing to go and

die for what he believed and then that dude backed off out of respect.

That's the kind of man that I strive to be everyday inside and outside

of the pimping game. I want to be like my father protecting his family.

Thanks for reading this book. I really hope that you got something out

of it. This is a very valuable piece of information that I sincerely hope

that you found educational as well as entertaining.

Look for more books that will be coming in the future about this here

pimping game. There are many more lessons to be learned.

And I look forward to being your teacher.

www.ingramcontent.com/pod-product-compliance
Lightning Source LLC
Chambersburg PA
CBHW081509250726
48662CB00021B/3033